POEMS ABOUT WAR

ROBERT GRAVES

POEMS ABOUT WAR

Edited with a commentary by
WILLIAM GRAVES

MOYER BELL LIMITED
MOUNT KISCO, NEW YORK & LONDON

Published by Moyer Bell Limited

First American Edition, 1990

**LIBRARY OF CONGRESS
CATALOGING-IN-PUBLICATION DATA**

Graves, Robert, 1895–1985
Poems about war / Robert Graves.—1st ed.
    p. cm.
    Includes bibliographical references.
    ISBN 1–55921–030–3 (paperback)

    1. World War, 1914–1918—Poetry. 2. War
poetry, English.
I. Title

PR6013.R35A6   1990
821'.912—dc20   90–38534
                                                      CIP

Printed in the United States of America
Distributed by Rizzoli

CONTENTS

INTRODUCTION

ROBERT GRAVES was nineteen years old in 1914 when he joined the Royal Welch Fusiliers. He rose to the rank of captain and was demobilized in 1919. On 20 July 1916 he was wounded and reported dead. He suffered from shell-shock for several years after the war.

Graves is among the sixteen poets of World War I commemorated on the stone in Poets' Corner, Westminster Abbey. However, he himself rejected all his war poems after 1927, and no examples of the period appear in his later collections of poems. I feel that the time has come to allow the poems by which he became known as a war poet to be reprinted.

I have included all Graves' completed war poems I could find, and have made no attempt at selection. Some are previously unpublished, some are drafts which he sent off from the trenches. Some he rejected almost immediately, some he was still satisfied with ten years after publication. The poems are, therefore, uneven. Eventually, all were suppressed when the war and its effects on him had passed. Then, after several years, he wrote 'Recalling War' and republished two of his early poems in a substantially altered form.

Alternating with his Georgian poetry, most of the poems appeared in *Over the Brazier* (1916), *Goliath and David* (privately printed 1916), *Fairies and Fusiliers* (1917), and in *Country Sentiment* (1920). About a third of the war poems reappeared in his *Collected Poems 1914–1926* (1927). Of those published up to 1927, only 'Sergeant-Major Money' was reprinted and then in a very different form. 'Recalling War' was written in 1938, when the mental wounds had healed. He suppressed it after 1961. 'Armistice Day, 1918' was published on the 49th anniversary of the event, and is the only war poem which appears in *Collected Poems 1975*. However, the first draft was written in 1918. I have included five previously unpublished poems; there may be others I am unaware of. For those who are interested, I have added bibliographical notes showing where each poem was published, and the variants it went through before it was suppressed.

The excerpt from Graves' article 'The Poets of World War II', under the heading 'Poetry of World War I', partly explains his attitude to war poetry. For background to his war experiences, his friendship with Siegfried Sassoon and other of the war poets, and with Sir Edward Marsh, editor of *Georgian Poetry*, who helped him to publish *Over the Brazier*, I would refer the reader to Graves' autobiography *Goodbye to All That*.

In 1927 he included his own selection of the war poems under the heading of 'War 1914–1919' in his *Collected Poems 1914–1926*. These are marked with an asterisk in the Contents. The notes printed under the poem headings appeared in the original editions. The footnotes I have added and are mostly Graves' annotations pencilled in his library copy of *Over the Brazier*. Others are from letters by Graves or from the first edition of *Goodbye to All That* (London: Jonathan Cape, 1929). Notes in brackets are my own.

I wish to thank Beryl Graves, Catherine Dalton, Sally Chilver and Pauline Scudamore for their help in preparing this collection. I am grateful to the Henry W. and Albert A. Berg Collection at the New York Public Library, Astor, Lenox and Tilden Foundations, for their kind co-operation in supplying copies of Graves' letters to Sir Edward Marsh and to Siegfried Sassoon which are in their possession. I am also grateful to the Poetry/Rare Books Collection, University Libraries, SUNY at Buffalo, for supplying copies of poems from the manuscripts in the Robert Graves Collection.

William Graves
Deya 1988

'POETRY OF WORLD WAR I'
BY ROBERT GRAVES

THE WAR-POETRY boom in World War I began with the death on active service of an R.N.V.R. sub-lieutenant, Rupert Brooke. The newspapers which had slated him as an impudent undergraduate versifier when his first poems were published a few months before, now paid him heroic honours. The sonnets in which he declared himself ready to die for an ideal England—rather than for the 'rolling ee' and 'jimp middle' of some Annie Laurie—were held to set a moral standard for young British manhood. They were not the only such poems written in 1914: 'Into Battle' by Julian Grenfell, a young Lancer officer, expressed the sudden overwhelming sense of natural beauty which a soldier is entitled to recognize as a premonition of death; Grenfell was killed in France shortly afterwards. And Charles Sorley, a twenty-year-old captain in the Suffolks—promotion was quick in those days—wrote:

> All the hills and dales along
> Earth is bursting into song . . .
>
> Earth that bore with joyful ease
> Hemlock for Socrates,
> Earth that blossomed and was glad
> 'Neath the cross that Christ had,
> Shall rejoice and blossom too
> When the bullet reaches you . . .
> So sing, marching men,
> Till the valleys ring again.

Sorley was killed at Loos in October, 1915.

War poetry at first had a resolute, self-dedicatory tone but, as the war settled down to a trench deadlock, self-dedication became qualified by homesick regrets for the lovely English countryside, away from all the mud, blood and desolation— the theme of mud, blood and desolation being more and more realistically treated. The close connexion between war poetry and Georgian poetry must be emphasized: there was a contrastive interplay between the horrors of trench warfare and the joys of simple bucolic experience. Georgian poetry, in the derogatory sense now always applied to it, was bucolic joy which lost its poignancy when the war eventually ended.

When war poetry became a fashion in 1915, a good deal of it was written imitatively by civilians who regretted that age or unfitness prevented them from also 'making the supreme sacrifice'. (I notice that Stephen Spender in an article on the subject has accidentally included one of these civilians, Wilfred Gibson, among the dead soldier heroes.) Also, many soldiers wrote as though they had seen more of the war than they really had. Robert Nichols, for instance, whose brief and uneventful service in France with the Royal Field Artillery was ended by sickness, published an exciting and apparently autobiographical poem, 'Attack', about the feelings of an infantry platoon commander in a trench battle; and one of the realistic war poems for which I was best known in those days, 'It's a Queer Time', was written at my regimental depot in Wales some weeks before I had a chance of verifying my facts.

By 1917 war poems were being published by the thousand. A typical anthology was E. B. Osborn's bulky *Muse in Arms,* with authors drawn from almost every regiment or corps in the Army—all very gallant and idealistic but with hardly a poet among them. War poetry was a major export to the United States. Robert Nichols scored a great success there as a crippled warrior, reading Siegfried Sassoon's poems, mine, and his own to university and women's club audiences; and when the United States finally came into the war, two American Rupert Brookes were found, Joyce Kilmer and Alan Seegar. 'I have a Rendezvous with Death' and 'Trees' were as widely popularized as Brooke's 'If I should die, think only this of me' and 'Grantchester'.

The character of British war poetry changed again in 1917, though what may be called the rank-and-file of war poets kept to the existing formulas. One of the two chief reasons for this was a realization by the more intelligent poets that the General Staff were sacrificing hundreds of thousands of lives in nightmare attacks which had no military justification; the other was the Conscription Act. Hitherto we had all been volunteers, and this had somehow been a consolation for the frightful conditions which trench warfare now implied. To be cannon-fodder was dispiriting enough: to have perhaps unwilling conscripts foisted on our company was worse still. Siegfried Sassoon, a Royal Welch Fusilier, had begun as a typical war poet with:

> Return to me, colours that were my joy,
> Not in the woeful crimson of men slain . . .

written before he went to France. Now he was an angry veteran, raging sarcastically at the stupidity, callousness, incompetence and hypocrisy of the men who were running the war; and even taking the line that it ought to be stopped as soon as possible by a negotiated peace, and that the Germans were not the only people to blame. In July, 1917, badly wounded and shell-shocked, he refused to serve further in the Army, and later recanted only because he felt that he was being a traitor to the men left in France. I was his escort to the shell-shock hospital near Edinburgh to which he was committed, where we met for the first time the war poet whose name is always linked with his—Wilfred Owen. Owen had been invalided home from the Manchester Regiment in France as of no further use to them. The mental rhythm of the typical war-neurosis was one of jagged ups and downs: the up-curves represented a despairing nervous energy which, when converted to poetic use, resulted in poems terrifyingly beyond the patient's normal capacity; the troughs meant listless, inept melancholia. Owen recovered, returned to France, won a Military Cross, and was killed just before the Armistice. Sassoon also returned to France and was again wounded in the head; but survived and wrote me a letter in verse beginning: 'I'd timed my death in action to the minute . . .' which I quote in the first edition of my *Goodbye to All That*.

(From 'War Poetry in This War', The Listener *23 October 1940, reprinted as* 'The Poets of World War II' *in* The Common Asphodel *(1949).)*

ON FINDING MYSELF A SOLDIER

My bud was backward to unclose,
  A pretty baby-queen,
Furled petal-tips of creamy rose
  Caught in a clasp of green.

Somehow, I never thought to doubt
  That when her heart should show
She would be coloured in as out,
  Like the flush of dawn on snow:

But yesterday aghast I found,
  Where last I'd left the bud,
Twelve flamy petals ringed around
  A heart more red than blood.

I was serving in France and had no leisure for getting the final proofs altogether as I wanted them. The same year, but too late, I decided on several alterations in the text, including the suppression of two small poems. *(From the Foreword to the 1920 edition of* Over the Brazier. *This poem and 'A Renascence' were the two in question.)*

THE SHADOW OF DEATH

Here's an end to my art!
  I must die and I know it,
With battle murder at my heart—
  Sad death for a poet!

Oh my songs never sung,
  And my plays to darkness blown!
I am still so young, so young,
  And life was my own.

Some bad fairy stole
  The baby I nursed:
Was this my pretty little soul,
  This changeling accursed?

To fight and kill is wrong—
  To stay at home wronger:
Oh soul, little play and song,
  I may father no longer!

La Bourse P-de.C., May 1915

(Place and date added in RG's library copy of Over the Brazier. *P-de.C. stands for* Pas de Calais.)

A RENASCENCE

White flabbiness goes brown and lean,
  Dumpling arms are now brass bars,
They've learnt to suffer and live clean,
  And to think below the stars.

They've steeled a tender, girlish heart,
  Tempered it with a man's pride,
Learning to play the butcher's part
  Though the woman screams inside—

Learning to leap the parapet,
  Face the open, rush, and then
To stab with the stark bayonet,
  Side by side with fighting men.

On Achi Baba's rock their bones
  Whiten, and on Flanders' plain,
But of their travailings and groans
  Poetry is born again.

(See note to 'On Finding Myself a Soldier'.)

THE MORNING BEFORE THE BATTLE

To-day, the fight: my end is very soon,
   And sealed the warrant limiting my hours:
I knew it walking yesterday at noon
   Down a deserted garden full of flowers.
. . . Carelessly sang, pinned roses on my breast,
   Reached for a cherry-bunch—and then, then, Death
Blew through the garden from the North and East
   And blighted every beauty with chill breath.

I looked, and ah, my wraith before me stood,
   His head all battered in by violent blows:
The fruit between my lips to clotted blood
   Was transubstantiate, and the pale rose
Smelt sickly, till it seemed through a swift tear-flood
   That dead men blossomed in the garden-close.

A garden in Béthune near the College des Jeunes Filles. (*RG's library copy of* Over the Brazier.)

LIMBO

After a week spent under raining skies,
   In horror, mud and sleeplessness, a week
Of bursting shells, of blood and hideous cries
   And the ever-watchful sniper: where the rcek
Of death offends the living . . . but poor dead
   Can't sleep, must lie awake with the horrid sound
That roars and whirs and rattles overhead
   All day, all night, and jars and tears the ground;
When rats run, big as kittens: to and fro
   They dart, and scuffle with their horrid fare,
And then one night relief comes, and we go
   Miles back into the sunny cornland where
Babies like tickling, and where tall white horses
Draw the plough leisurely in quiet courses.

Vieux Bergum, 1915

THE TRENCHES
(Heard in the Ranks)

Scratches in the dirt?
No, that sounds much too nice.
Oh, far too nice.
Seams, rather, of a Greyback Shirt,
And we're the little lice
Wriggling about in them a week or two,
Till one day, suddenly, from the blue
Something bloody and big will come
Like—watch this fingernail and thumb!—
Squash! and he needs no twice.

(NURSERY MEMORIES)
I — THE FIRST FUNERAL
*(The first corpse I saw was on the
German wires, and couldn't be buried)*

The whole field was so smelly;
   We smelt the poor dog first:
His horrid swollen belly
   Looked just like going burst.

His fur was most untidy;
   He hadn't any eyes.
It happened on Good Friday
   And there was lots of flies.

And then I felt the coldest
   I'd ever felt, and sick,
But Rose, 'cause she's the oldest,
   Dared poke him with her stick.

He felt quite soft and horrid:
   The flies buzzed round his head
And settled on his forehead:
   Rose whispered: 'That dog's dead.

'You bury all dead people,
   When they're quite really dead,
Round churches with a steeple:
   Let's bury this,' Rose said.

'And let's put mint all round it
   To hide the nasty smell.'
I went to look and found it —
   Lots, growing near the well.

We poked him through the clover
   Into a hole, and then
We threw brown earth right over
   And said: 'Poor dog, Amen!'

This incident was at Harlech in 1899 at the end of Sandy Road crossing the
Golf Links. (*RG's library copy of* Over the Brazier.)

II—THE ADVENTURE
(Suggested by the claim of a machine-gun team to
have annihilated an enemy wire party: no bodies
were found however)

To-day I killed a tiger near my shack
Among the trees: at least, it must have been,
Because his hide was yellow, striped with black,
    And his eyes were green.

I crept up close and slung a pointed stone
With all my might: I must have hit his head,
For there he died without a twitch or groan,
    And he lay there dead.

I expect that he'd escaped from a Wild Beast Show
By pulling down his cage with an angry tear;
He'd killed and wounded all the people—so
    He was hiding there.

I brought my brother up as quick's I could
But there was nothing left when he did come:
The tiger's mate was watching in the wood
    And she'd dragged him home.

But, anyhow, I killed him by the shack,
'Cause—listen!—when we hunted in the wood
My brother found my pointed stone all black
    With the clotted blood.

(NURSERY MEMORIES)
III—I HATE THE MOON
(After a moonlight patrol near the Brickstacks)

I hate the Moon, though it makes most people glad,
    And they giggle and talk of silvery beams—you know!
But *she* says the look of the Moon drives people mad,
    And that's the thing that always frightens me so.

I hate it worst when it's cruel and round and bright,
    And you can't make out the marks on its stupid face,
Except when you shut your eyelashes, and all night
    The sky looks green, and the world's a horrible place.

I like the stars, and especially the Big Bear
    And the W star, and one like a diamond ring,
But I *hate* the Moon and its horrible stony stare,
    And I know one day it'll do me some dreadful thing.

August 1915

With Sergeant Williams of the 2nd R.W.Fus., B. Coy. Killed in 1916 in a raid at Cambrin. (*RG's library copy of* Over the Brazier.)

BIG WORDS

'I've whined of coming death, but now, no more!
It's weak and most ungracious. For, say I,
Though still a boy if years are counted, why!
I've lived those years from roof to cellar-floor,
And feel, like grey-beards touching their fourscore,
Ready, so soon as the need comes, to die:
    And I'm satisfied.
For winning confidence in those quiet days
Of peace, poised sickly on the precipice side
Of Lliwedd crag by Snowdon, and in war
Finding it firmlier with me than before;
Winning a faith in the wisdom of God's ways
That once I lost, finding it justified
Even in this chaos; winning love that stays
And warms the heart like wine at Easter tide;
    Having earlier tried
False loves in plenty; oh! my cup of praise
Brims over, and I know I'll feel small sorrow,
Confess no sins and make no weak delays
If death ends all and I must die to-morrow.'

But on the firestep, waiting to attack,
He cursed, prayed, sweated, wished the proud words back.

July 1915

The postscript was added after Loos. (*RG's library copy of* Over the Brazier.)

THE DEAD FOX HUNTER

*(In memory of Captain A. L. Samson, 2nd Battalion
Royal Welch Fusiliers, killed near Cuinchey,
Sept. 25th, 1915)*

We found the little captain at the head;
 His men lay well aligned.
We touched his hand—stone cold—and he was dead,
 And they, all dead behind,
Had never reached their goal, but they died well;
They charged in line, and in the same line fell.

The well-known rosy colours of his face
 Were almost lost in grey.
We saw that, dying and in hopeless case,
 For others' sake that day
He'd smothered all rebellious groans: in death
His fingers were tight clenched between his teeth.

For those who live uprightly and die true
 Heaven has no bars or locks,
And serves all taste . . . or what's for him to do
 Up there, but hunt the fox?
Angelic choirs? No, Justice must provide
For one who rode straight and in hunting died.

So if Heaven had no Hunt before he came,
 Why, it must find one now:
If any shirk and doubt they know the game,
 There's one to teach them how:
And the whole host of Seraphim complete
Must jog in scarlet to his opening Meet.

IT'S A QUEER TIME

It's hard to know if you're alive or dead
When steel and fire go roaring through your head.

One moment you'll be crouching at your gun
Traversing, mowing heaps down half in fun:
The next, you choke and clutch at your right breast
No time to think—leave all—and off you go . . .
To Treasure Island where the Spice winds blow,
To lovely groves of mango, quince and lime—
Breathe no goodbye, but ho, for the Red West!
        It's a queer time.

You're charging madly at them yelling 'Fag!'
When somehow something gives and your feet drag.
You fall and strike your head; yet feel no pain
And find . . . you're digging tunnels through the hay
In the Big Barn, 'cause it's a rainy day.
Oh springy hay, and lovely beams to climb!
You're back in the old sailor suit again.
        It's a queer time.

Or you'll be dozing safe in your dug-out—
A great roar—the trench shakes and falls about—
You're struggling, gasping, struggling, then . . . hullo!
Elsie comes tripping gaily down the trench,
Hanky to nose—that lyddite makes a stench—
Getting her pinafore all over grime.
Funny! because she died ten years ago!
        It's a queer time.

The trouble is, things happen much too quick;
Up jump the Boches, rifles thump and click,
You stagger, and the whole scene fades away:
Even good Christians don't like passing straight
From Tipperary or their Hymn of Hate
To Alleluiah-chanting, and the chime
Of golden harps . . . and . . . I'm not well to-day . . .
    It's a queer time.

May 1915

Written as a matter of fact just before I went out to France, at Wrexham.
(RG's library copy of Over the Brazier.)

1915

I've watched the Seasons passing slow, so slow,
In the fields between La Bassée and Béthune;
Primroses and the first warm day of Spring,
Red poppy floods of June,
August, and yellowing Autumn, so
To Winter nights knee-deep in mud or snow,
And you've been everything,

Dear, you've been everything that I most lack
In these soul-deadening trenches—pictures, books,
Music, the quiet of an English wood,
Beautiful comrade-looks,
The narrow, bouldered mountain-track,
The broad, full-bosomed ocean, green and black,
And Peace, and all that's good.

Written at Havre in the winter of 1915. *(RG's library copy of* Over the
Brazier.)

OVER THE BRAZIER

What life to lead and where to go
   After the War, after the War?
   We'd often talked this way before,
But I still see the brazier glow
That April night, still feel the smoke
And stifling pungency of burning coke.

I'd thought: 'A cottage in the hills,
   North Wales, a cottage full of books,
   Pictures and brass and cosy nooks
And comfortable broad window-sills,
Flowers in the garden, walls all white.
I'd live there peacefully and dream and write.'

But Willie said; 'No, Home's no good:
   Old England's quite a hopeless place,
   I've lost all feeling for my race:
But France has given my heart and blood
Enough to last me all my life,
I'm off to Canada with my wee wife.'

'Come with us, Mac, old thing,' but Mac
   Drawled; 'No, a Coral Isle for me,
   A warm green jewel in the South Sea.
There's merit in a lumber shack,
And labour is a grand thing . . . but—
Give me my hot beach and my cocoanut.'

So then we built and stocked for Willie
   His log-hut, and for Mac a calm
   Rock-a-bye cradle on a palm—
Idyllic dwellings—but this silly
Mad War has now wrecked both, and what
Better hopes has my little cottage got?

1915

With the 2nd Welsh Regiment at Vermelles, 1915. *(RG's library copy of* Over the Brazier.)

THE BOUGH OF NONSENSE
(An Idyll)

Back from the Somme two Fusiliers
Limped painfully home; the elder said,
S. 'Robert, I've lived three thousand years
This Summer, and I'm nine parts dead.'
R. 'But if that's truly so,' I cried, 'quick, now,
Through these great oaks and see the famous bough

'Where once a nonsense built her nest
With skulls and flowers and all things queer,
In an old boot, with patient breast
Hatching three eggs; and the next year . . .'
S. 'Foaled thirteen squamous young beneath, and rid
Wales of drink, melancholy, and psalms, she did.'

Said he, 'Before this quaint mood fails,
We'll sit and weave a nonsense hymn,'
R. 'Hanging it up with monkey tails
In a deep grove all hushed and dim . . .'
S. 'To glorious yellow-bunched banana-trees,'
R. 'Planted in dreams by pious Portuguese,'

S. 'Which men are wise beyond their time,
And worship nonsense, no one more.'
R. 'Hard by, among old quince and lime,
They've built a temple with no floor,'
S. 'And whosoever worships in that place
He disappears from sight and leaves no trace.'

R. 'Once the Galatians built a fane
To Sense: what duller God than that?'
S. 'But the first day of autumn rain
The roof fell in and crushed them flat.'
R. 'Ay, for a roof of subtlest logic falls
When nonsense is foundation for the walls.'

I tell him old Galatian tales;
He caps them in quick Portuguese,
While phantom creatures with green scales
Scramble and roll among the trees.
The hymn swells; on a bough above us sings
A row of bright pink birds, flapping their wings.

13 August 1916

GOLIATH AND DAVID
*(For Lieut. David Thomas, 1st Batt. Royal
Welch Fusiliers, killed at Fricourt, March, 1916)*

'If I am Jesse's son,' said he,
'Where must that tall Goliath be?'
For once an earlier David took
Smooth pebbles from the brook:
Out between the lines he went
To that one-sided tournament,
A shepherd boy who stood out fine
And young to fight a Philistine
Clad all in brazen mail. He swears
That he's killed lions, he's killed bears,
And those that scorn the God of Zion
Shall perish so like bear or lion.
But . . . the historian of that fight
Had not the heart to tell it right.

Striding within javelin range,
Goliath marvels at this strange
Goodly-faced boy so proud of strength.
David's clear eye measures the length;
With hand thrust back, he cramps one knee,
Poises a moment thoughtfully,
And hurls with a long vengeful swing.
The pebble, humming from the sling
Like a wild bee, flies a sure line
For the forehead of the Philistine;
Then . . . but there comes a brazen clink,
And quicker than a man can think
Goliath's shield parries each cast,
Clang! clang! And clang! was David's last.

Scorn blazes in the Giant's eye,
Towering unhurt six cubits high.
Says foolish David, 'Curse your shield!
And curse my sling! but I'll not yield.'
He takes his staff of Mamre oak,
A knotted shepherd-staff that's broke
The skull of many a wolf and fox
Come filching lambs from Jesse's flocks.
Loud laughs Goliath, and that laugh
Can scatter chariots like blown chaff
To rout; but David, calm and brave,
Holds his ground, for God will save.
Steel crosses wood, a flash, and oh!
Shame for beauty's overthrow!
(God's eyes are dim, His ears are shut),
One cruel backhand sabre-cut—
'I'm hit! I'm killed!' young David cries,
Throws blindly forward, chokes . . . and dies.
Steel-helmeted and grey and grim
Goliath straddles over him.

THE LAST POST
(On Sick Leave)

The bugler sent a call of high romance—
'Lights out! Lights out!' to the deserted square.
On the thin brazen notes he threw a prayer,
'God, if it's *this* for me next time in France . . .
O spare the phantom bugle as I lie
Dead in the gas and smoke and roar of guns,
Dead in a row with the other broken ones
Lying so stiff and still under the sky,
Jolly young Fusiliers too good to die.'

A DEAD BOCHE

To you who'd read my songs of War
　And only hear of blood and fame,
I'll say (you've heard it said before)
　'War's Hell!' and if you doubt the same,
To-day I found in Mametz Wood
A certain cure for lust of blood:

Where, propped against a shattered trunk,
　In a great mess of things unclean,
Sat a dead Boche; he scowled and stunk
　With clothes and face a sodden green,
Big-bellied, spectacled, crop-haired,
Dribbling black blood from nose and beard.

13 July 1915

I went into the wood to find German overcoats to use as blankets. Mametz Wood was full of dead of the Prussian Guards Reserve, big men, and of Royal Welch and South Wales Borderers of the new-army battalions, little men. There was not a single tree in the wood unbroken. I got my greatcoats and came away as quickly as I could, climbing over the wreckage of green branches. Going and coming, by the only possible route, I had to pass by the corpse of a German with his back propped against a tree. He had a green face, spectacles, close shaven hair; black blood was dripping from the nose and beard. He had been there for some days and was bloated and stinking. (Goodbye to All That, *p. 264*.)

ESCAPE

*(August 6th, 1916—Officer previously reported died
of wounds, now reported wounded.
Graves, Captain R., Royal Welch Fusiliers)*

. . . But I *was* dead, an hour or more.
I woke when I'd already passed the door
That Cerberus guards, and half-way down the road
To Lethe, as an old Greek signpost showed.
Above me, on my stretcher swinging by,
I saw new stars in the subterrene sky:
A Cross, a Rose in bloom, a Cage with bars,
And a barbed Arrow feathered in fine stars.
I felt the vapours of forgetfulness
Float in my nostrils. Oh, may Heaven bless
Dear Lady Proserpine, who saw me wake,
And, stooping over me, for Henna's sake
Cleared my poor buzzing head and sent me back
Breathless, with leaping heart along the track.
After me roared and clattered angry hosts
Of demons, heroes, and policeman-ghosts.
'Life! life! I can't be dead! I won't be dead!
Damned if I'll die for anyone!' I said . . .
Cerberus stands and grins above me now,
Wearing three heads—lion, and lynx, and sow.
Quick, a revolver! But my Webley's gone,
Stolen . . . No bombs . . . no knife . . . The crowd
      swarms on,
Bellows, hurls stones . . . Not even a honeyed sop . . .
Nothing . . . Good Cerberus! . . . Good dog! . . .
      but stop!
Stay! . . . A great luminous thought . . . I do believe
There's still some morphia that I bought on leave.
Then swiftly Cerberus' wide mouths I cram
With army biscuit smeared with ration jam;
And sleep lurks in the luscious plum and apple.
He crunches, swallows, stiffens, seems to grapple
With the all-powerful poppy . . . then a snore,
A crash; the beast blocks up the corridor
With monstrous hairy carcase, red and dun—
Too late! for I've sped through.
            O Life! O Sun!

31

NOT DEAD

Walking through trees to cool my heat and pain,
I know that David's with me here again.
All that is simple, happy, strong, he is.
Caressingly I stroke
Rough bark of the friendly oak.
A brook goes bubbling by: the voice is his.
Turf burns with pleasant smoke;
I laugh at chaffinch and at primroses.
All that is simple, happy, strong, he is.
Over the whole wood in a little while
Breaks his slow smile.

'Not Dead' I wrote in France about poor David Thomas. *(Letter to Marsh, 4 April 1916.)*

THE LEGION

'Is that the Three-and-Twentieth, Strabo mine,
Marching below, and we still gulping wine?'
From the sad magic of his fragrant cup
The red-faced old centurion started up,
Cursed, battered on the table. 'No,' he said,
'Not that! The Three-and-Twentieth Legion's dead,
Dead in the first year of this damned campaign —
The Legion's dead, dead, and won't rise again.
Pity? Rome pities her brave lads that die,
But we need pity also, you and I,
Whom Gallic spear and Belgian arrow miss,
Who live to see the Legion come to this,
Unsoldierlike, slovenly, bent on loot,
Grumblers, diseased, unskilled to thrust or shoot.
O brown cheek, muscled shoulder, sturdy thigh!
Where are they now? God! watch it straggle by,
The sullen pack of ragged ugly swine.
Is that the Legion, Gracchus? Quick, the wine!'
'Strabo,' said Gracchus, 'you are strange to-night.
The Legion is the Legion, it's all right.
If these new men are slovenly, in your thinking,
Hell take it! you'll not better them by drinking.
They all try, Strabo; trust their hearts and hands.
The Legion is the Legion while Rome stands
And these same men before the autumn's fall
Shall bang old Vercingetorix out of Gaul.'

Late 1916

TO LUCASTA ON GOING TO THE WARS—
FOR THE FOURTH TIME

It doesn't matter what's the cause,
   What wrong they say we're righting,
A curse for treaties, bonds and laws,
   When we're to do the fighting!
And since we lads are proud and true,
   What else remains to do?
Lucasta, when to France your man
Returns his fourth time, hating war,
Yet laughs as calmly as he can
   And flings an oath, but says no more,
That is not courage, that's not fear—
Lucasta he's a Fusilier,
   And his pride sends him here.

Let statesmen bluster, bark and bray
   And so decide who started
This bloody war, and who's to pay
   But he must be stout-hearted,
Must sit and stake with quiet breath,
   Playing at cards with Death.
Don't plume yourself he fights for you;
It is no courage, love, or hate
That lets us do the things we do;
   It's pride that makes the heart so great;
It is not anger, no, nor fear—
Lucasta he's a Fusilier,
   And his pride keeps him here.

TWO FUSILIERS

And have we done with War at last?
Well, we've been lucky devils both,
And there's no need of pledge or oath
To bind our lovely friendship fast,
By firmer stuff
Close bound enough.

By wire and wood and stake we're bound,
By Fricourt and by Festubert,
By whipping rain, by the sun's glare,
By all the misery and loud sound,
By a Spring day,
By Picard clay.

Show me the two so closely bound
As we, by the wet bond of blood,
By friendship blossoming from mud,
By Death: we faced him, and we found
Beauty in Death,
In dead men, breath.

TO R. N.
*(From Frise on the Somme in
February 1917, in answer to a
letter, saying: 'I am just
finishing my "Faun" poem:
I wish you were here to feed
him with cherries.')*

Here by a snow-bound river
In scrapen holes we shiver,
And like old bitterns we
Boom to you plaintively;
Robert, how can I rhyme
Verses at your desire—
Sleek fauns and cherry-time,
Vague music and green trees,
Hot sun and gentle breeze,
England in June attire,
And life born young again,
For your gay goatish brute
Drunk with warm melody
Singing on beds of thyme
With red and rolling eye,
Waking with wanton lute
All the Devonian plain,
Lips dark with juicy stain,
Ears hung with bobbing fruit?
Why should I keep him time?
Why in this cold and rime,
Where even to dream is pain?
No, Robert, there's no reason;
Cherries are out of season,
Ice grips at branch and root,
And singing birds are mute.

DEAD COW FARM

An ancient saga tells us how
In the beginning the First Cow
(For nothing living yet had birth
But elemental Cow on Earth)
Began to lick cold stones and mud:
Under her warm tongue flesh and blood
Blossomed, a miracle to believe;
And so was Adam born, and Eve.
Here now is chaos once again,
Primæval mud, cold stones and rain.
Here flesh decays and blood drips red,
And the Cow's dead, the old Cow's dead.

SORLEY'S WEATHER

When outside the icy rain
   Comes leaping helter-skelter,
Shall I tie my restive brain
   Snugly under shelter?

Shall I make a gentle song
   Here in my firelit study,
When outside the winds blow strong
   And the lanes are muddy?

With old wine and drowsy meats
   Am I to fill my belly?
Shall I glutton here with Keats?
   Shall I drink with Shelley?

Tobacco's pleasant, firelight's good:
   Poetry makes both better.
Clay is wet and so is mud,
   Winter rains are wetter.

Yet rest there, Shelley, on the sill,
   For though the winds come frorely
I'm away to the rain-blown hill
   And the ghost of Sorley.

WHEN I'M KILLED

When I'm killed, don't think of me
Buried there in Cambrin Wood,
Nor as in Zion think of me
With the Intolerable Good.
And there's one thing that I know well,
I'm damned if I'll be damned to Hell!

So when I'm killed, don't wait for me,
Walking the dim corridor;
In Heaven or Hell, don't wait for me,
Or you must wait for evermore.
You'll find me buried, living-dead
In these verses that you've read.

So when I'm killed, don't mourn for me.
Shot, poor lad, so bold and young,
Killed and gone—don't mourn for me.
On your lips my life is hung:
O friends and lovers, you can save
Your playfellow from the grave.

FAMILIAR LETTER TO SIEGFRIED SASSOON
(From Bivouacs at Mametz Wood,
July 13th, 1916)

I never dreamed we'd meet that day
In our old haunts down Fricourt way,
Plotting such marvellous journeys there
For golden-houred 'Après-la-guerre.'

Well, when it's over, first we'll meet
At Gweithdy Bach, my country seat
In Wales, a curious little shop
With two rooms and a roof on top,
A sort of Morlancourt-ish billet
That never needs a crowd to fill it.
But oh, the country round about!
The sort of view that makes you shout
For want of any better way
Of praising God: there's a blue bay
Shining in front, and on the right
Snowdon and Hebog capped with white,
And lots of other mountain peaks
That you could wonder at for weeks,
With jag and spur and hump and cleft.
There's a grey castle on the left,
And back in the high hinterland
You'll see the grave of Shawn Knarlbrand
Who slew the savage Buffaloon
By the Nant-col one night in June,
And won his surname from the horn
Of this prodigious unicorn.
Beyond, where the two Rhinogs tower,
Rhinog Fach and Rhinog Fawr,
Close there after a four years' chase
From Thessaly and the woods of Thrace,
The beaten Dog-cat stood at bay
And growled and fought and passed away.
You'll see where mountain conies grapple
With prayer and creed in their rock chapel
Which three young children built for them;
They call it Söar Bethlehem.
You'll see where in old Roman days,

Before Revivals changed our ways,
The Virgin 'scaped the Devil's grab,
Printing her foot on a stone slab
With five clear toe-marks; and you'll find
The fiendish thumb-print close behind.
You'll see where Math, Mathonwy's son,
Spoke with the wizard Gwydion
And bad him for South Wales set out
To steal that creature with the snout,
That new-discovered grunting beast
Divinely flavoured for the feast.
No traveller yet has hit upon
A wilder land than Meirion,
For desolate hills and tumbling stones,
Bogland and melody and old bones.
Fairies and ghosts are here galore,
And poetry most splendid, more
Than can be written with the pen
Or understood by common men

In Gweithdy Bach we'll rest a while,
We'll dress our wounds and learn to smile
With easier lips; we'll stretch our legs,
And live on bilberry tart and eggs,
And store up solar energy,
Basking in sunshine by the sea,
Until we feel a match once more
For *anything* but another war.
So then we'll kiss our families,
And sail away across the seas
(The God of Song protecting us)
To the great hills of Caucasus.
Robert will learn the local *bat*
For billeting and things like that,
If Siegfried learns the piccolo
To charm the people as we go.
The simple peasants clad in furs
Will greet the foreign officers
With open arms, and ere they pass
Will make them tuneful with Kavasse.
In old Bagdad we'll call a halt
At the Sashuns' ancestral vault;

We'll catch the Persian rose-flowers' scent,
And understand what Omar meant.
Bitlis and Mush will know our faces,
Tiflis and Tomsk, and all such places.
Perhaps eventually we'll get
Among the Tartars of Thibet,
Hobnobbing with the Chungs and Mings,
And doing wild, tremendous things
In free adventure, quest and fight,
And God! what poetry we'll write!

THE NEXT WAR

You young friskies who to-day
Jump and fight in Father's hay
With bows and arrows and wooden spears,
Playing at Royal Welch Fusiliers,
Happy though these hours you spend,
Have they warned you how games end?
Boys, from the first time you prod
And thrust with spears of curtain-rod,
From the first time you tear and slash
Your long-bows from the garden ash,
Or fit your shaft with a blue jay feather,
Binding the split tops together,
From that same hour by fate you're bound
As champions of this stony ground,
Loyal and true in everything,
To serve your Army and your King,
Prepared to starve and sweat and die
Under some fierce foreign sky,
If only to keep safe those joys
That belong to British boys,
To keep young Prussians from the soft
Scented hay of father's loft,
And stop young Slavs from cutting bows
And bendy spears from Welsh hedgerows.
    Another War soon gets begun,
A dirtier, a more glorious one;
Then, boys, you'll have to play, all in;
It's the cruellest team will win.
So hold your nose against the stink
And never stop too long to think.
Wars don't change except in name;
The next one must go just the same,
And new foul tricks unguessed before
Will win and justify this War.
Kaisers and Czars will strut the stage
Once more with pomp and greed and rage;
Courtly ministers will stop
At home and fight to the last drop;
By the million men will die
In some new horrible agony;

And children here will thrust and poke,
Shoot and die, and laugh at the joke,
With bows and arrows and wooden spears,
Playing at Royal Welch Fusiliers.

A CHILD'S NIGHTMARE

Through long nursery nights he stood
By my bed unwearying,
Loomed gigantic, formless, queer,
Purring in my haunted ear
That same hideous nightmare thing,
Talking, as he lapped my blood,
In a voice cruel and flat,
Saying for ever, 'Cat! . . . Cat! . . . Cat! . . .'

That one word was all he said,
That one word through all my sleep,
In monotonous mock despair.
Nonsense may be light as air
But there's Nonsense that can keep
Horror bristling round the head,
When a voice cruel and flat
Says for ever, 'Cat! . . . Cat! . . . Cat! . . .'

He had faded, he was gone
Years ago with Nursery Land,
When he leapt on me again
From the clank of a night train,
Overpowered me foot and hand
Lapped my blood, while on and on
The old voice cruel and flat
Purred for ever, 'Cat! . . . Cat! . . . Cat! . . .'

Morphia drowsed, again I lay
In a crater by High Wood:
He was there with straddling legs,
Staring eyes as big as eggs,
Purring as he lapped my blood,
His black bulk darkening the day,
With a voice cruel and flat,
'Cat! . . . Cat! . . . Cat! . . .' he said,
    'Cat! . . . Cat! . . .'

When I'm shot through heart and head,
And there's no choice but to die,
The last word I'll hear, no doubt,
Won't be 'Charge!' or 'Bomb them out!'
Nor the stretcher-bearer's cry,
'Let that body be, he's dead!'
But a voice cruel and flat
Saying for ever, 'Cat! . . . Cat! . . . Cat!'

CORPORAL STARE

Back from the line one night in June,
I gave a dinner at Béthune —
Seven courses, the most gorgeous meal
Money could buy or batman steal.
Five hungry lads welcomed the fish
With shouts that nearly cracked the dish;
Asparagus came with tender tops,
Strawberries in cream, and mutton chops.
Said Jenkins, as my hand he shook,
'They'll put this in the history book.'
We bawled Church anthems *in choro*
Of Bethlehem and Hermon snow,
With drinking-songs, a mighty sound
To help the good red Pommard round.
Stories and laughter interspersed,
We drowned a long La Bassée thirst —
Trenches in June make throats damned dry.
Then through the window suddenly,
Badge, stripes and medals all complete,
We saw him swagger up the street,
Just like a live man — Corporal Stare!

Stare! Killed last month at Festubert,
Caught on patrol near the Boche wire,
Torn horribly by machine-gun fire!
He paused, saluted smartly, grinned,
Then passed away like a puff of wind,
Leaving us blank astonishment.
The song broke, up we started, leant
Out of the window—nothing there,
Not the least shadow of Corporal Stare,
Only a quiver of smoke that showed
A fag-end dropped on the silent road.

I saw a ghost at Béthune. He was a man called Private Challoner who had
been at Lancaster with me and again in F company at Wrexham. When he
went out with a draft to join the First Battalion he shook my hand and said:
'I'll meet you again in France, sir.' He had been killed at Festubert in May
and in June he passed by our C Company billet where we were just having a
special dinner to celebrate our safe return from Cuinchy. There was fish,
new potatoes, green peas, asparagus, mutton chops, strawberries and
cream, and three bottles of Pommard. Challoner looked in at the window,
saluted and passed on. There was no mistaking him or the cap-badge he was
wearing. There was no Royal Welch battalion billeted within miles of
Béthune at the time. I jumped up and looked out of the window, but saw
nothing except a fag-end smoking on the pavement. Ghosts were numerous
in France at the time. (Goodbye to All That, *p. 161.*)

'THE ASSAULT HEROIC'

Down in the mud I lay,
Tired out by my long day
Of five damned days and nights,
Five sleepless days and nights . . .
Dream snatched, and set me where
The dungeon of Despair
Looms over Desolate Sea,
Frowning and threatening me
With aspect high and steep—
A most malignant keep.
My foes that lay within
Shouted and made a din,
Hooted and grinned and cried:
'To-day we've killed your pride;
To-day your ardour ends.
We've murdered all your friends;
We've undermined by stealth
Your happiness and your health.
We've taken away your hope;
Now you may droop and mope
To misery and to death.'
But with my spear of faith,
Stout as an oaken rafter,
With my round shield of laughter,
With my sharp, tongue-like sword
That speaks a bitter word,
I stood beneath the wall
And there defied them all.
The stones they cast I caught
And alchemized with thought
Into such lumps of gold
As dreaming misers hold.
The boiling oil they threw,
Fell in a shower of dew,
Refreshing me; the spears
Flew harmless by my ears,
Struck quivering in the sod;
There, like the prophet's rod,
Put leaves out, took firm root,
And bore me instant fruit.

My foes were all astounded,
Dumbstricken and confounded,
Gaping in a long row;
They dared not thrust nor throw.
Thus, then, I climbed a steep
Buttress and won the keep,
And laughed and proudly blew
My horn, *'Stand to! Stand to!*
Wake up, sir! Here's a new
Attack! Stand to! Stand to!'

THROUGH THE PERISCOPE

Trench stinks of shallow buried dead
  Where Tom stands at the periscope,
Tired out. After nine months he's shed
  All fear, all faith, all hate, all hope.

Sees with uninterested eye
  Beyond the barbed wire, a gay bed
Of scarlet poppies and the lie
  Of German trench behind that red —

Six poplar trees . . . a rick . . . a pond
  A ruined hamlet and a mine . . .
More trees, more houses and beyond
  La Bassée spire in gold sunshine.

The same thoughts always haunt his brain,
  Two sad, one scarcely comforting,
First second third and then again
  The first and the second silly thing.

The first 'It's now nine months and more
  That I've drunk British beer', the second
'The last few years of this mad war
  Will be the cushiest, I've reckoned'

The third 'The silly business is
  I'll only die in the next war,
Suppose by luck I get through this,
  Just 'cause I wasn't killed before.'

Quietly he laughs, and at that token
  The first thought should come round again
But crack!
        The weary circle's broken
  And a bullet tears through the tired brain.

1915

DIED OF WOUNDS

And so they marked me dead, the day
That I turned twenty-one?
They counted me as dead, did they,
The day my childhood slipped away
And manhood was begun?
Oh, that was fit and that was right!
Now, Daddy Time, with all your spite,
Buffet me how you can,
You'll never make a man of me
For I lie dead in Picardy,
Rather than grow to man.
Oh that was the right day to die
The twenty-fourth of July!
God smiled
Beguiled
By a wish so wild,
And let me always stay a child.

I wrote the following silly thing last night in a moment of abstraction and I have made it into the shape of a funeral urn. (*In a letter to Marsh, 18 October 1916.*)

THE SAVAGE STORY OF CARDONETTE

To Cardonette, to Cardonette,
   Back from the Marne the Boches came
With hearts like lead, with feet that bled
   To Cardonette in the morning.

They hurry fast through Cardonette:
   No time to stop or ask the name,
No time to stop or rape or shoot
   In Cardonette, this morning.

They hurry fast through Cardonette,
   But close behind with eyes of flame
The Turco steals upon their heels
   Through Cardonette in the morning.

And half a mile from Cardonette,
   He caught those Boches tired and lame,
He charged and broke their ranks like smoke
   By Cardonette in the morning.

At Cardonette, at Cardonette,
   He taught the Boche a pretty game:
He cut off their ears for souvenirs
   At Cardonette in the morning.

14 August 1916

The only first-hand account I heard of large-scale atrocities was from an old woman at Cardonette on the Somme, with whom I was billeted in July 1916. It was at Cardonette that a battalion of French Turcos overtook the rear guard of a German division retreating from the Marne in September 1914. The Turcos surprised the dead-weary Germans while they were still marching in column. The old woman went, with gestures, through a pantomime of slaughter, ending: 'Et enfin, ces animaux leur ont arraché les oreilles et les ont mis à la poche.' The presence of coloured troops in Europe was, from the German point of view, we knew, one of the chief Allied atrocities. (Goodbye to All That, *p. 237. A Turco was one of a body of native Algerian light infantry in the French Army.)*

THE PATCHWORK QUILT

Here is this patchwork quilt I've made
Of patterned silks and old brocade,
Small faded rags in memory rich
Sewn each to each with feather stitch,
But if you stare aghast perhaps
At certain muddied khaki scraps
Or trophy-fragments of field grey,
Clotted and torn, a grim display
That never decked white sheets before,
Blame my dazed head, blame bloody war.

It shall be called 'The Patchwork Quilt' I think, with an explanation perhaps of
this kind: *(The poem followed. Letter to Sassoon, 9 July 1918, in reference to a
book of poems* [The Patchwork Flag, *not published*] *he was getting together.)*

TRENCH LIFE

Fear never dies, much as we laugh at fear
    For pride's sake and for other cowards' sakes,
And when we see some new Death, bursting near,
    Rip those that laugh in pieces, God! it shakes
Sham fortitude that went so proud at first,
    And stops the clack of mocking tongues awhile
Until (o pride, pride!) at the next shell-burst
    Cowards dare mock again and twist a smile.

Yet we who once, before we came to fight,
    Drowned our prosperity in a waste of grief,
Contrary now find such perverse delight
    In utter fear and misery, that Belief
Blossoms from mud, and under the rain's whips,
Flagellant-like we writhe with laughing lips.

HAUNTED

Gulp down your wine, old friends of mine,
Roar through the darkness, stamp and sing
And lay ghost hands on everything,
But leave the noonday's warm sunshine
To living lads for mirth and wine.

I met you suddenly down the street,
Strangers assume your phantom faces,
You grin at me from daylight places,
Dead, long dead, I'm ashamed to greet
Dead men down the morning street.

RETROSPECT: THE JESTS OF THE CLOCK

He had met hours of the clock he never guessed before—
Dumb, dragging, mirthless hours confused with dreams and
    fear,
Bone-chilling, hungry hours when the Gods sleep and snore,
Bequeathing earth and heaven to ghosts, and will not hear,
And will not hear man groan chained to the sodden ground,
Rotting alive; in feather beds they slumbered sound.

When noisome smells of day were sicklied by cold night,
When sentries froze and muttered; when beyond the wire
Blank shadows crawled and tumbled, shaking, tricking the
    sight,
When impotent hatred of Life stifled desire,
Then soared the sudden rocket, broke in blanching showers,
O lagging watch! O dawn! O hope-forsaken hours!

How often with numbed heart, stale lips, venting his rage
He swore he'd be a dolt, a traitor, a damned fool,
If, when the guns stopped, ever again from youth to age
He broke the early rising, early sleeping rule.
No, though more bestial enemies roused a fouler war
Never again would he hear this, no never more!

'Rise with the cheerful sun, go to bed with the same,
Work in your field or kailyard all the shining day,
But,' he said, 'never more in quest of wealth, honour, fame,
Search the small hours of night before the East goes grey.
A healthy mind, an honest heart, a wise man leaves
Those ugly impious times to ghosts, devils, soldiers, thieves.'

Poor fool, knowing too well deep in his heart
That he'll be ready again: if urgent orders come,
To quit his rye and cabbages, kiss his wife and part
At the first sullen rapping of the awakened drum,
Ready once more to sweat with fear and brace for the shock,
To greet beneath a falling flare the jests of the clock.

HERE THEY LIE

Here they lie who once learned here
   All that is taught of hurt or fear;
Dead, but by free will they died:
   They were true men, they had pride.

TOM TAYLOR

On pay-day nights, neck-full with beer,
Old soldiers stumbling homeward here,
Homeward (still dazzled by the spark
Love kindled in some alley dark)
Young soldiers mooning in slow thought,
Start suddenly, turn about, are caught
By a dancing sound, merry as a grig,
Tom Taylor's piccolo playing jig.
Never was blown from human cheeks
Music like this, that calls and speaks
Till sots and lovers from one string
Dangle and dance in the same ring.
Tom, of your piping I've heard said
And seen—that you can rouse the dead,
Dead-drunken men awash who lie
In stinking gutters hear your cry,
I've seen them twitch, draw breath, grope, sigh,
Heave up, sway, stand; grotesquely then
You set them dancing, these dead men.
They stamp and prance with sobbing breath,
Victims of wine or love or death,
In ragged time they jump, they shake
Their heads, sweating to overtake
The impetuous tune flying ahead.
They flounder after, with legs of lead.
Now, suddenly as it started, play
Stops, the short echo dies away,
The corpses drop, a senseless heap
The drunk men gaze about like sheep.

Grinning, the lovers sigh and stare
Up at the broad moon hanging there,
While Tom, five fingers to his nose,
Skips off . . . And the last bugle blows.

There was a boy called Taylor in my company. He had been at Lancaster, and I had bought him a piccolo to play when the detachment went out on route-marches; he would give us one tune after another for mile after mile. The other fellows carried his pack and rifle. At Wrexham, on pay-nights, he used to sit in the company billet, which was the drill-hall near the station, and play jigs for the drunks to dance to. He never drank himself. The music was slow at first, but he gradually quickened it until he worked them into a frenzy. He would delay this climax until my arrival with the company orderly-sergeant. The sergeant would fling open the door and bellow: 'F Company, Attention!' Taylor would break off, thrust the piccolo under his blankets, and spring to his feet. The drunks were left frozen in the middle of their capers, blinking stupidly. (Goodbye to All That, *p. 112*).

COUNTRY AT WAR

And what of home—how goes it, boys,
While we die here in stench and noise?
'The hill stands up and hedges wind
Over the crest and drop behind;
Here swallows dip and wild things go
On peaceful errands to and fro
Across the sloping meadow floor,
And make no guess at blasting war.
In woods that fledge the round hill-shoulder
Leaves shoot and open, fall and moulder,
And shoot again. Meadows yet show
Alternate white of drifted snow
And daisies. Children play at shop,
Warm days, on the flat boulder-top,
With wildflower coinage, and the wares
Are bits of glass and unripe pears.
Crows perch upon the backs of sheep,
The wheat goes yellow: women reap,
Autumn winds ruffle brook and pond,
Flutter the hedge and fly beyond.
So the first things of nature run,
And stand not still for any one,
Contemptuous of the distant cry
Wherewith you harrow earth and sky.
And high French clouds, praying to be
Back, back in peace beyond the sea,
Where nature with accustomed round
Sweeps and garnishes the ground
With kindly beauty, warm or cold—
Alternate seasons never old:
Heathen, how furiously you rage,
Cursing this blood and brimstone age,
How furiously against your will
You kill and kill again, and kill:
All thought of peace behind you cast,
Till like small boys with fear aghast,
Each cries for God to understand,
"I could not help it, it was my hand." '

SOSPAN FACH
(The Little Saucepan)

Four collier lads from Ebbw Vale
Took shelter from a shower of hail,
And there beneath a spreading tree
Attuned their mouths to harmony.

With smiling joy on every face
Two warbled tenor, two sang bass,
And while the leaves above them hissed with
Rough hail, they started 'Aberystwyth'.

Old Parry's hymn, triumphant, rich,
They changed through with even pitch,
Till at the end of their grand noise
I called: 'Give us the "Sospan" boys!'

Who knows a tune so soft, so strong,
So pitiful as that 'Saucepan' song
For exiled hope, despaired desire
Of lost souls for their cottage fire?

Then low at first with gathering sound
Rose their four voices, smooth and round,
Till back went Time: once more I stood
With Fusiliers in Mametz Wood.

Fierce burned the sun, yet cheeks were pale,
For ice hail they had leaden hail;
In that fine forest, green and big,
There stayed unbroken not one twig.

They sang, they swore, they plunged in haste,
Stumbling and shouting through the waste;
The little 'Saucepan' flamed on high,
Emblem of hope and ease gone by.

Rough pit-boys from the coaly South,
They sang, even in the cannon's mouth;
Like Sunday's chapel, Monday's inn,
The death-trap sounded with their din.

*   *   *   *   *

The storm blows over, Sun comes out,
The choir breaks up with jest and shout,
With what relief I watch them part—
Another note would break my heart!

THE LEVELLER

Near Martinpuisch that night of hell
Two men were struck by the same shell,
Together tumbling in one heap
Senseless and limp like slaughtered sheep.

One was a pale eighteen-year-old,
Blue-eyed and thin and not too bold,
Pressed for the war ten years too soon,
The shame and pity of his platoon.

The other came from far-off lands
With bristling chin and whiskered hands,
He had known death and hell before
In Mexico and Ecuador.

Yet in his death this cut-throat wild
Groaned 'Mother! Mother!' like a child,
While that poor innocent in man's clothes
Died cursing God with brutal oaths.

Old Sergeant Smith, kindest of men,
Wrote out two copies there and then
Of his accustomed funeral speech
To cheer the womenfolk of each:—

'He died a hero's death: and we
His comrades of 'A' Company
Deeply regret his death: we shall
All deeply miss so true a pal.'

HATE NOT, FEAR NOT

Kill if you must, but never hate:
  Man is but grass and hate is blight,
The sun will scorch you soon or late,
  Die wholesome then, since you must fight.

Hate is a fear, and fear is rot
  That cankers root and fruit alike,
Fight cleanly then, hate not, fear not,
  Strike with no madness when you strike.

Fever and fear distract the world,
  But calm be you though madmen shout,
Through blazing fires of battle hurled,
  Hate not, strike, fear not, stare Death out!

A RHYME OF FRIENDS
(In a Style Skeltonical)

Listen now this time
Shortly to my rhyme
That herewith starts
About certain kind hearts
In those stricken parts
That lie behind Calais,
Old crones and aged men
And young childrén.
About the Picardais,
Who earned my thousand thanks,
Dwellers by the banks
Of mournful Somme
(God keep me therefrom
Until War ends) —
These, then, are my friends:
Madame Averlant Lune,
From the town of Béthune;
Good Professeur la Brune
From that town also.
He played the piccolo,
And left his locks to grow.
Dear Madame Hojdés,
Sempstress of Saint Fé.
With Jules and Susette
And Antoinette.
Her children, my sweethearts,
For whom I made darts
Of paper to throw
In their mimic show,
'La guerre aux tranchées.'
That was a pretty play.

There was old Jacques Caron,
Of the hamlet Mailleton.
He let me look
At his household book,
'Comment vivre cent ans.'
What cares I took
To obey this wise book,
I, who feared each hour
Lest Death's cruel power
On the poppied plain
Might make cares vain!

By Nœux-les-mines
Lived old Adelphine,
Withered and clean,
She nodded and smiled,
And used me like a child.
How that old trot beguiled
My leisure with her chatter,
Gave me a china platter
Painted with Cherubim
And mottoes on the rim.
But when instead of thanks
I gave her francs
How her pride was hurt!
She counted francs as dirt,
(God knows, she was not rich)
She called the Kaiser bitch,
She spat on the floor,
Cursing this Prussian war,
That she had known before
Forty years past and more.

There was also 'Tomi',
With looks sweet and free,
Who called me *cher ami.*
This orphan's age was nine,
His folk were in their graves,
Else they were slaves
Behind the German line
To terror and rapine —
O, little friends of mine
How kind and brave you were,
You smoothed away care
When life was hard to bear.
And you, old women and men,
Who gave me billets then,
How patient and great-hearted!
Strangers though we started,
Yet friends we ever parted.
God bless you all: now ends
This homage to my friends.

Instead of children as a way of forgetting the war, I used Nancy. *Country Sentiment* dedicated to her, was a collection of romantic poems and ballads. At the end was a group of pacifist war-poems. It contained one about the French civilians — I cannot think how I came to put so many lies in it — I even said that old Adelphine Heu of Annezin gave me a painted china plate, and that her pride was hurt when I offered to pay her. The truth is that I bought the plate from her for about fifteen shillings and that I never got it from her. Adelphine's daughter-in-law would not allow her to give it up, claiming it as her own, and I never got my money back from Adelphine. (Goodbye to All That, *p. 342.*)

OTHER

SERGEANT-MAJOR MONEY

It wasn't our battalion, but we lay alongside it,
   So the story is as true as the telling is frank.
They hadn't one Line-officer left, after Arras,
   Except a batty major and the Colonel, who drank.

'B' Company Commander was fresh from the Depôt,
   An expert on gas drill, otherwise a dud;
So Sergeant-Major Money carried on, as instructed,
   And that's where the swaddies began to sweat blood.

His Old Army humour was so well-spiced and hearty
   That one poor sod shot himself, and one lost his wits;
But discipline's maintained, and back in rest-billets
   The Colonel congratulates 'B' company on their kits.

The subalterns went easy, as was only natural
   With a terror like Money driving the machine,
Till finally two Welshmen, butties from the Rhondda,
   Bayoneted their bugbear in a field-canteen.

Well, we couldn't blame the officers, they relied on Money;
   We couldn't blame the pitboys, their courage was grand;
Or, least of all, blame Money, an old stiff surviving
   In a New (bloody) Army he couldn't understand.

1917

PEACE

When that glad day shall break to match
'Before-the-War' with 'Since-the-Peace',
And up I climb to twist new thatch
Across my cottage roof, while geese
Stand stiffly there below and vex
The yard with hissing from long necks,
In that immense release,.
That shining day, shall we hear said:
'New wars to-morrow, more men dead'?

When peace time comes and horror's over,
Despair and darkness like a dream,
When fields are ripe with corn and clover,
The cool white dairy full of cream,
Shall we work happily in the sun,
And think 'It's over now and done,'
Or suddenly shall we seem
To watch a second bristling shadow
Of armed men move across the meadow?

Will it be over once for all,
With no more killed and no more maimed;
Shall we be safe from terror's thrall,
The eagle caged, the lion tamed;
Or will the young of that vile brood,
The young ones also, suck up blood
Unconquered, unashamed,
Rising again with lust and thirst?
Better we all had died at first,
Better that killed before our prime
  We rotted deep in earthy slime.

Summer 1918

BAZENTIN, 1916
(A Reminiscence — Robert and David)

R. That was a curious night two years ago,
   Relieving those tired Dockers at Bazentin.
   Remember climbing up between the ruins?
   The guide that lost his head when the gas-shells came,
   Lurching about this way and that, half-witted,
   Till we were forced to find the way ourselves?

D. Yes, twilight torn with flashes, faces muffled,
   In stinking masks, and eyes all sore and crying
   With lachrymatory stuff, and four men gassed.

R. Yet we got up there safely, found the trenches
   Untraversed shallow ditches, along a road
   With dead men sprawled about, some ours, some theirs —

D. Ours mostly, and those Dockers doing nothing,
   Tired out, poor devils; much too tired to dig,
   Or to do anything but just hold the ground:
   No touch on either flank, no touch in front,
   Everything in the air. I cursed, I tell you.
   Out went the Dockers, quick as we filed in,
   And soon we'd settled down and put things straight,
   Posted the guns, dug in, got out patrols,
   And sent to right and left to restore touch.

R. There was a sunken road out on the right,
   With rifle-pits half dug; at every pit
   A dead man had his head thrust in for shelter.

D. Dawn found us happy enough; a funny day —
   The strangest I remember in all those weeks.
   German five-nines were bracketting down our trenches
   Morning and afternoon.

R.   Why, yes; at dinner,
   Three times my cup was shaken out of my hand
   And filled with dirt: I had to pour out fresh.

D. That was the mug you took from the Boche gun.
Remember that field gun, with the team killed
By a lucky shot just as the German gunners
Were limbering up? We found the gunner's treasures
In a box behind, his lump of fine white chalk
Carefully carved, and painted with a message
Of love to his dear wife, and Allied flags,
A list of German victories, and an eagle.
Then his clean washing, and his souvenirs—
British shell-heads, French bullets, lumps of shrapnel,
Nothing much more. I never thought it lucky
To take that sort of stuff.

R.   Then a tame magpie—
German, we guessed—came hopping into the trench,
Picking up scraps of food. That's 'One for sorrow'
I said to little Owen.

D.   Not much mistaken
In the event, when only three days later
They threw us at High Wood and (mind, we got there!)
Smashed up the best battalion in the whole corps.
But, Robert, quite the queerest thing that day
Happened in the late afternoon. Worn out,
I snatched two hours of sleep; the Boche bombardment
Roared on, but I commended my soul to God,
And slept half through it; but as I lay there snoring
A mouse, in terror of all these wild alarms,
Crept down my neck for shelter, and woke me up
In a great sweat. Blindly I gave one punch
And slew the rascal at the small of my back.
That was a strange day!

R.   Yes, and a merry one.

1918

ARMISTICE DAY, 1918

What's all this hubbub and yelling,
  Commotion and scamper of feet,
With ear-splitting clatter of kettles and cans,
  Wild laughter down Mafeking Street?

O, those are the kids whom we fought for
  (You might think they'd been scoffing our rum)
With flags that they waved when we marched off to war
  In the rapture of bugle and drum.

Now they'll hang Kaiser Bill from a lamp-post,
  Von Tirpitz they'll hang from a tree . . .
We've been promised a 'Land Fit for Heroes'—
  What heroes we heroes must be!

And the guns that we took from the Fritzes,
  That we paid for with rivers of blood,
Look, they're hauling them down to Old Battersea Bridge
  Where they'll topple them, souse, in the mud!

But there's old men and women in corners
  With tears falling fast on their cheeks,
There's the armless and legless and sightless—
  It's seldom that one of them speaks.

And there's flappers gone drunk and indecent
  Their skirts kilted up to the thigh,
The constables lifting no hand in reproof
  And the chaplain averting his eye . . .

When the days of rejoicing are over,
  When the flags are stowed safely away,
They will dream of another wild 'War to End Wars'
  And another wild Armistice day.

But the boys who were killed in the trenches,
  Who fought with no rage and no rant,
We left them stretched out on their pallets of mud
  Low down with the worm and the ant.

1918

AN OCCASION

'The trenches are filled in, the houseless dead
Disperse and on the rising thunder-storm
Cast their weak limbs, are whirled up overhead
In clouds of fear . . .'
                  Then suddenly as you read,
As we sat listening there, and cushioned warm,
War-scarred yet safe, alive beyond all doubt,
The blundering gale outside faltered, stood still:
Two bolts clicked at the glass doors, and a shrill
Impetuous gust of wind blew in with a shout,
Fluttering your poems. And the lamp went out.

1920

71

A LETTER FROM WALES
(Richard Rolls to his friend, Captain Abel Wright)

This is a question of identity
Which I can't answer. Abel, I'll presume
On your good-nature, asking you to help me.
I hope you will, since you too are involved
As deeply in the problem as myself.
Who are we? Take down your old diary, please,
The one you kept in France, if you *are* you
Who served in the Black Fusiliers with me.
That is, again, of course, if I am I —
This isn't Descartes' philosophic doubt,
But, as I say, a question of identity,
And practical enough — Turn up the date,
July the twenty-fourth, nineteen-sixteen,
And read the entry there:
                    'To-day I met
Meredith, transport-sergeant of the Second.
He told me that Dick Rolls had died of wounds.
I found out Doctor Dunn, and he confirms it;
Dunn says he wasn't in much pain, he thinks.'

Then the first draft of a verse-epitaph,
Expanded later into a moving poem.
'Death straddled on your bed: you groaned and tried
To stare him out, but in that death-stare died.'
Yes, died, poor fellow, the day he came of age.
But then appeared a second Richard Rolls
(Or that's the view that the facts force on me),
Showing Dick's features to support his claim
To rank and pay and friendship, Abel, with you.
And you acknowledged him as the old Dick,
Despite all evidence to the contrary,
Because, I think, you missed the dead too much.
You came up here to Wales to stay with him
And I don't know for sure, but I suspect
That you were dead too, killed at the Rectangle
One bloody morning of the same July,
The time that something snapped and sent you Berserk:
You ran across alone, with covering fire
Of a single rifle, routing the Saxons out

With bombs and yells and your wild eye; and stayed there
In careless occupation of the trench
For a full hour, reading, by all that's mad,
A book of pastoral poems! Then, they say,
Then you walked slowly back and went to sleep
Without reporting; that was the occasion,
No doubt, they killed you: it was your substitute
Strolled back and laid him down and woke as you,
Showing your features to support his claim
To rank and pay and friendship, Abel, with me.
So these two substitutes, yours and my own
(Though that's an Irish way of putting it,
For the I now talking is an honest I,
Independent of the I's now lost,
And a live dog's as good as a dead lion),
So, these two friends the second of the series,
Came up to Wales pretending a wild joy
That they had cheated Death: they stayed together
At the same house and ate and drank and laughed
And wrote each other's poems, much too lazy
To write their own, and sat up every night
Talking and smoking almost until dawn.
Yes, they enjoyed life, but unless I now
Confound my present feeling, with the past,*
They felt a sense of unreality
In the proceedings—stop! that's good, *proceedings,*
It suggests ghosts.—Well, then I want to ask you
Whether it really happened. Eating, laughing,
Sitting up late, writing each other's verses,
I might invent all that, but one thing happened
That seems too circumstantial for romance.
Can you confirm it? Yet, even if you can,
What does that prove? for who are you? or I?
Listen, it was a sunset. We were out
Climbing the mountain, eating blackberries;
Late afternoon, the third week in September,
The date's important: it might prove my point,
For unless Richard Rolls had really died
Could he have so recovered from his wounds
As to go climbing less than two months later?

---

*A reminiscence from Wordsworth's 'Nutting'. *(Graves' footnote to poem)*

And if it comes to that, what about you?
How had you come on sick-leave from the Line?
I don't remember you, that time, as wounded.
Anyhow . . . We were eating blackberries
By a wide field of tumbled boulderstones
Hedged with oaks and nut-trees. Gradually
A glamour spread about us, the low sun
Making the field unreal as a stage,
Gilding our faces with heroic light:
Then oaks and nut-boughs caught this golden flood,
Sending it back in a warm flare of green . . .
There was a mountain-ash among the boulders,
But too full-clustered and symmetrical
And highly coloured to convince as real.
We stopped blackberrying and someone said
(Was it I or you?) 'It is good for us to be here.'
The other said, 'Let us build Tabernacles.'
(In honour of a new Transfiguration;
It was that sort of moment); but instead
I climbed up on the massive pulpit stone,
An old friend, but unreal with the rest,
And prophesied—not indeed of the future,
But declaimed poetry, and you climbed up too
And prophesied. The next thing I remember
Was a dragon scaly with fine-weather clouds
Poised high above the sun, and the sun dwindling
And then the second glory.
                              You'll remember
That we were not then easily impressed
With pyrotechnics, whether God's or man's.
We had seen the sun rise daily, weeks on end,
And watched the nightly rocket-shooting, varied
With red and green, and livened with gun-fire
And the loud single-bursting overgrown squib
Thrown from the minen-werfer: and one night
From a billet-window some ten miles away
We had watched the French making a mass-attack
At Notre Dame de Lorette, in a thunderstorm.

That was a grand display of all the Arts,
God's, Man's, the Devil's: in the course of which,
So lavishly the piece had been stage-managed,

A Frenchman was struck dead by a meteorite,
That was the sort of gala-show it was!
But this Welsh sunset, what shall I say of it?
It ended not at all as it began,
An influence rather than a spectacle
Raised to a strange degree beyond all wonder.
And I remember that we looked and found
A region of the sky below the dragon
Where we could gaze behind all time and space
And see as it were the colour of pure thought,
The texture of emptiness, and at that sight
We came away, not daring to see more:
Death was the price, we knew, of such perfection;
And walking home . . .

                 fell in with Captain Todd,
The Golf-Club Treasurer; he greeted us
With '*Did* you see that splendid sunset, boys?
Magnificent, was it not? I wonder now,
What writer could have done real justice to it
Except, of course, my old friend Walter Pater?
Ruskin perhaps? Yes, Ruskin might have done it.'

Well, *did* that happen, or am I just romancing?
And then again, one has to ask the question
What happened after to that *you* and *me*?
I have thought lately that they too got lost.
My representative went out once more
To France, and so did yours, and yours got killed,
Shot through the throat while bombing up a trench
At Bullecourt; if not there, then at least
On the thirteenth of July, nineteen eighteen,
Somewhere in the neighbourhood of Albert,
When you took a rifle bullet through the skull
Just after breakfast on a mad patrol.
But still you kept up the same stale pretence
As children do in nursery battle-games,
'No, I'm not dead. Look, I'm not even wounded.'
And I admit I followed your example,
Though nothing much happened that time in France.
I died at Hove after the Armistice,
Pneumonia, with the doctor's full consent.

I think the I and you who then took over
Rather forgot the part we used to play;
We wrote and saw each other often enough
And sent each other copies of new poems,
But there was a constraint in all our dealings,
A doubt, unformulated, but quite heavy
And not too well disguised. Something we guessed
Arising from the War, and yet the War
Was a forbidden ground of conversation.
Now *why,* can you say *why,* short of accepting
My substitution view? Then yesterday,
After five years of this relationship,
I found a relic of the second Richard,
A pack-valise marked with his name and rank . . .
And a sunset started, most unlike the other,
A pink-and-black depressing sort of show
Influenced by the Glasgow School of Art.
It sent me off on a long train of thought
And I began to feel badly confused,
Being accustomed to this newer self;
I wondered whether you could reassure me.
Now I have asked you, do you see my point?
What I'm asking really isn't 'Who am I?'
Or, 'Who are you?' (you see my difficulty?)
But a stage before that, '*how am I to put
The question that I'm asking you to answer?*'

c.1924

A DEDICATION OF THREE HATS

This round hat I devote to Mars,
   Tough steel with leather lined.
My skin's my own, redeemed by scars
From further still more futile wars
   The god may have in mind.

Minerva takes my square of black
   Well tasselled with the same;
Her dullest nurselings never lack
With hoods of scarlet at their back
   And letters to their name.

But this third hat, the foolscap sheet,
   (For there's a strength in three)
Unblemished, conical and neat
I hang up here without deceit
   To kind Euphrosyne.

Goddess, accept with smiles or tears
   This gift of a gross fool
Who having sweated in death fears
With wounds and cramps for three long years
   Limped back, and sat for school.

c.1919

RECALLING WAR

Entrance and exit wounds are silvered clean,
The track aches only when the rain reminds.
The one-legged man forgets his leg of wood,
The one-armed man his jointed wooden arm.
The blinded man sees with his ears and hands
As much or more than once with both his eyes.
Their war was fought these twenty years ago
And now assumes the nature-look of time,
As when the morning traveller turns and views
His wild night-stumbling carved into a hill.

What, then, was war? No mere discord of flags
But an infection of the common sky
That sagged ominously upon the earth
Even when the season was the airiest May.
Down pressed the sky, and we, oppressed, thrust out
Boastful tongue, clenched fist and valiant yard.
Natural infirmities were out of mode,
For Death was young again: patron alone
Of healthy dying, premature fate-spasm.

Fear made fine bed-fellows. Sick with delight
At life's discovered transitoriness,
Our youth became all-flesh and waived the mind.
Never was such antiqueness of romance,
Such tasty honey oozing from the heart.
And old importances came swimming back —
Wine, meat, log-fires, a roof over the head,
A weapon at the thigh, surgeons at call.
Even there was a use again for God —
A word of rage in lack of meat, wine, fire,
In ache of wounds beyond all surgeoning.

War was return of earth to ugly earth,
War was foundering of sublimities,
Extinction of each happy art and faith
By which the world had still kept head in air,
Protesting logic or protesting love,
Until the unendurable moment struck —
The inward scream, the duty to run mad.

And we recall the merry ways of guns—
Nibbling the walls of factory and church
Like a child, piecrust; felling groves of trees
Like a child, dandelions with a switch.
Machine-guns rattle toy-like from a hill,
Down in a row the brave tin-soldiers fall:
A sight to be recalled in elder days
When learnedly the future we devote
To yet more boastful visions of despair.

c.1938

ADDENDUM: THE PATCHWORK FLAG

The English Edition of *Poems About War* appeared in 1988, on the seventieth anniversary of Armistice Day. Since then I have found the typescript of a book of poems, *The Patchwork Flag*, prepared by Graves in 1918 but which he never published. 'The Patchwork Quilt' (p. 53), which Graves included in a letter to Sassoon announcing his project, became the 'Foreword' to the collection, the first line changing to:

> There is a patchwork lately made
> . . .

I wish to thank J.W.D. Hibberd for bringing it to my attention among the Sir Edward Marsh papers in the Henry W. and Albert A. Berg Collection at the New York Public Library. Although most of the poems in the typescript appeared in *Country Sentiment* and elsewhere, a dozen poems in the collection are unknown and, of these, four are war poems. Only a fragment of 'Letter to S.S. from Bryn-y-Pin,' which appears in a letter to Sassoon, has been published previously. Printing costs do not justify a 'New Edition' incorporating them in the main body of the book, but I have thought it pertinent to include them as an *addendum*.

William Graves
Deyá Mallorca, Spain
1990

LETTER TO S.S. FROM BRYN-Y-PIN

Poor Fusilier aggrieved with fate
That lets you lag in France so late,
When all our friends of two years past
Are free of trench and wire at last
Dear lads, one way or the other done
With grim-eyed War and homeward gone
Crippled with wounds or daft or blind,
Or leaving their dead clay behind,
Where still you linger, lone and drear,
Last of the flock, poor Fusilier.
Now your brief letters home pretend
Anger and scorn that this false friend
This fickle Robert whom you knew
To writhe once, tortured just like you,
By world-pain and bound impotence
Against all Europe's evil sense
Now snugly lurks at home to nurse
His wounds without complaint, and worse,
Preaches "The Bayonet" to Cadets
On a Welsh hill-side, grins, forgets.
That now he rhymes of trivial things
Children, true love and robins' wings
Using his tender nursery trick.
Though hourly yet confused and sick
From those foul shell-holes drenched in gas
The stumbling shades to Lethe pass—
"*Guilty*" I plead and by that token
Confess my haughty spirit broken
And my pride gone; now the least chance
Of backward thought begins a dance
Of marionettes that jerk cold fear
Against my sick mind: either ear
Rings with dark cries, my frightened nose
Smells gas in scent of hay or rose,
I quake dumb horror, till again
I view that dread La Bassée plain
Drifted with smoke and groaning under
The echoing strokes of rival thunder
That crush surrender from me now.
Twelve months ago, on an oak bough

81

I hung, absolved of further task,
My dinted helmet, my gas mask,
My torn trench tunic with grim scars
Of war; so tamed the wrath of Mars
With votive gifts and one short prayer.
"Spare me! Let me forget, O spare!"
"*Guilty*" I've no excuse to give
While in such cushioned ease I live
With Nancy and fresh flowers of June
And poetry and my young platoon,
Daring how seldom search behind
In those back cupboards of my mind
Where lurk the bogeys of old fear,
To think of you, to feel you near
By our old bond, poor Fusilier.

NIGHT MARCH

Evening: beneath tall poplar trees
    We soldiers eat and smoke and sprawl,
Write letters home, enjoy our ease,
    When suddenly comes a ringing call.

"Fall in!" A stir, and up we jump,
    Fold the love letter, drain the cup,
We toss away the Woodbine stump,
    Snatch at the pack and jerk it up.

Soon with a roaring song we start,
    Clattering along a cobbled road,
The foot beats quickly like the heart,
    And shoulders laugh beneath their load.

Where are we marching? No one knows,
    Why are we marching? No one cares.
For every man follows his nose,
    Towards the gay West where sunset flares.

An hour's march: we halt: forward again,
    Wheeling down a small road through trees.
Curses and stumbling: puddled rain
    Shines dimly, splashes feet and knees.

Silence, disquiet: from those trees
    Far off a spirit of evil howls.
"Down to the Somme" wail the banshees
    With the long mournful voice of owls.

The trees are sleeping, their souls gone,
    But in this time of slumbrous trance
Old demons of the night take on
    Their windy foliage, shudder and dance,

Out now: the land is bare and wide,
    A grey sky presses overhead.
Down to the Somme! In fields beside
    Our tramping column march the dead.

Our comrades who at Festubert
    And Loos and Ypres lost their lives
In dawn attacks, in noonday glare,
    On dark patrols from sudden knives.

Like us they carry packs, they march
    In fours, they sling their rifles too,
But long ago they've passed the arch
    Of death where we must yet pass through.

Seven miles: we halt awhile, then on!
    I curse beneath my burdening pack
Like Sinbad when with sigh and groan
    He bore the old man on his back.

A big moon shines across the road,
    Ten miles: we halt: now on again
Drowsily marching; the sharp goad
    Blunts to a dumb and sullen pain.

A man falls out; we others go
    Ungrudging on, but our quick pace
Full of hope once, grows dull, and slow:
    No talk: nowhere a smiling face.

Above us glares the unwinking moon,
    Beside us march the silent dead:
My train of thought runs mazy, soon
    Curious fragments crowd my head.

I puzzle old things learned at school,
    Half riddles, answerless, yet intense,
A date, an algebraic rule,
    A bar of music with no sense.

We win the fifteenth mile by strength
    "Halt!" the men fall, and where they fall,
Sleep. "On!" the road uncoils its length;
    Hamlets and towns we pass them all.

False dawn declares night nearly gone:
    We win the twentieth mile by theft.

We're charmed together, hounded on,
　　By the strong beat of left, right, left.

Pale skies and hunger: drizzled rain:
　　The men with stout hearts help the weak,
Add a new rifle to their pain
　　Of shoulder, stride on, never speak.

We win the twenty-third by pride:
　　My neighbour's face is chalky white.
Red dawn: a mocking voice inside
　　"New every morning", "Fight the good fight".

Now at the top of a rounded hill
　　We see brick buildings and church spires.
Nearer they loom and nearer, till
　　We know the billet of our desires.

Here the march ends, somehow we know.
　　The step quickens, the rifles rise
To attention: up the hill we go,
　　Shamming new vigour for French eyes.

So now most cheerily we step down
　　The street, scarcely withholding tears
Of weariness: so stir the town
　　With all the triumph of Fusiliers.

Breakfast to cook, billets to find,
　　Scrub up and wash (down comes the rain),
And the dark thought in every mind
　　"To-night they'll march us on again."

POETIC INJUSTICE

A Scottish fighting man whose wife
   Turned false and tempted his best friend,
Finding no future need for life
   Resolved he'd win a famous end.

Bayonet and bomb this wild man took,
   And Death in every shell-hole sought,
Yet there Death only made him hook
   To dangle bait that others caught.

A hundred German wives soon owed
   Their widows' weeds to this one man
Who also guided down Death's road
   Scores of the Scots of his own clan.

Seventeen wounds he got in all
   And jingling medals four or five.
Often in trenches at night-fall
   He was the one man left alive.

But fickle wife and paramour
   Were strangely visited from above,
Were light'ning-struck at their own door
   About the third week of their love.

"Well, well" you say, "man wife and friend
   Ended as quits" but I say not:
While that false pain met a clean end
   Without remorse, how fares the Scot?

THE SURVIVOR COMES HOME

Despair and doubt in the blood:
Autumn, a smell rotten-sweet:
What stirs in the drenching wood?
What drags at my heart, my feet?
What stirs in the wood?

Nothing stirs, nothing cries.
Run weazel, cry bird for me,
Comfort my ears, soothe my eyes!
Horror on ground, over tree!
Nothing calls, nothing flies.

Once in a blasted wood,
A shrieking fevered noise,
We jeered at Death where he stood:
I jeered, I too had a taste
Of death in the wood.

Am I alive and the rest
Dead, all dead? Sweet friends
With the sun they have journeyed west;
For me now night never ends,
A night without rest.

Death, your revenge is ripe.
Spare me! but can Death spare?
Must I leap, howl to your pipe
Because I denied you there?
Your vengeance is ripe.

Death, ay, terror of Death
If I laughed at you, scorned you now
You flash in my eyes, choke my breath
"Safe home." Safe? Twig and bough
Drip, drip, drip with Death!

BIBLIOGRAPHICAL NOTES

Graves' works are commonly identified by the 'Higginson reference'. The Higginson references below are taken from the second edition: *A Bibliography of the Writings of Robert Graves* by Fred H. Higginson, second edition revised by William Proctor Williams (St Pauls Bibliographies, 1987). The publications these references denote are also given below.

POEM	PUBLISHING HISTORY (HIGGINSON REF.)
On Finding Myself a Soldier	A1a only
The Shadow of Death	A1
A Renascence	A1a only
The Morning Before the Battle	A1; C36
Limbo	A1 (Mss extant)
The Trenches	A1
The First Funeral	A1 (Mss extant)
The Adventure	A1 (Mss extant)
I Hate the Moon	A1 (Mss extant)
Big Words	A1
The Dead Fox Hunter	A1, 23, 24; C37
It's a Queer Time	A1 (Mss extant)
1915	A1, 3, 23, 24; C35
Over the Brazier	A1, 23, 24
The Bough of Nonsense	A2, 3, 23, 24 (Mss extant)
Goliath and David	A2, 3, 23, 24
The Last Post	A2, 3, 23, 24; C40, 43, 49
A Dead Boche	A2, 3, (23, 24); C39
Escape	A2, 3, 17, 23, 24; C49 (Mss extant)
Not Dead	A2, 3, 23, 24; C41 (Mss extant)
The Legion	A3, 23, 24
To Lucasta on Going to the Wars	A3; C49
Two Fusiliers	A3, 23, 24
To R. N.	A3, 23, 24
Dead Cow Farm	A3, 23, 24; B1.1

PUBLICATIONS

A1a *Over the Brazier.* 1st ed., London: The Poetry Bookshop, 1 May 1916. (A photographic facsimile of the British Library copy was issued in 1975 by St James Press in London and St Martin's Press in New York.)

A1b *Over the Brazier.* 2nd ed., London: The Poetry Bookshop, May 1920.

A2   *Goliath and David.* Privately printed by Chiswick Press, London, late 1916.

A3   *Fairies and Fusiliers*. London: William Heinemann, 8 November 1917, and New York: Alfred Knopf, November 1918. (Norwood Editions published a photographic reprint in 1977.)

A5   *Country Sentiment*. London: Martin Secker, March 1920, and New York: Alfred Knopf, March 1920.

A16   *Welchman's Hose*. London: The Fleuron, September 1925. (A photocopy publication of this edition was issued by Folcroft Press in 1976.)

A17   *Robert Graves*. The Augustan Books of Modern Poetry Series, London: Ernest Benn, November 1925.

A23   *Poems (1914–1926)*, London: William Heinemann, 2 June 1927, and Garden City, New York: Doubleday, Doran & Co., 13 September 1929.

A24   *Poems (1914–1927)*. London: William Heinemann, June 1927. (A limited edition of A23 including some recent poems.)

A48   *Collected Poems*. London, Toronto, Melbourne, Sydney: Cassell, 16 March 1939.

A50   *No More Ghosts*. London: Faber & Faber, September 1940.

A58   *Poems 1938–1945*. London, Toronto, Melbourne, Sydney: Cassell, November 1945.

A60   *Collected Poems (1914–1947)*. London, Toronto, Melbourne, Sydney: Cassell, April 1948.

A73   *Collected Poems 1955*. Garden City, New York: Doubleday, 30 June 1955.

A83   *Poems Selected by Himself*. Harmondsworth: Penguin Books, 29 August 1957.

A85   *The Poems of Robert Graves*. Garden City, New York: Doubleday, Anchor Books, 5 June 1958.

A87   *Collected Poems 1959*. London: Cassell, 25 April 1959.

A94   *Selected Poetry and Prose*. Ed. James Reeves, London: Hutchinson Educational, 15 May 1961.

A95   *Collected Poems 1961*. Garden City, New York: Doubleday, 21 July 1961.

A114   *Collected Poems 1965*. London: Cassell, 23 September 1965.

A127   *Beyond Giving*. Privately printed by Stellar Press, Hatfield, 19 October 1969.

A129   *Poems 1968–1970*. London: Cassell, 12 October 1970.

A138 *Collected Poems 1975.* London: Cassell, September 1975, and Garden City, New York: Doubleday, January 1977.

B1.1 *Oxford Poetry 1917.* Oxford: Blackwell, November 1917.
B6   *Cenotaph.* Ed. Thomas Moult, London: Jonathan Cape, November 1923.

C35 *Westminster Gazette* 6 March 1916.
C36 *Westminster Gazette* 13 March 1916.
C37 *Westminster Gazette* 20 September 1916, and *Saturday Westminster Gazette* 23 September 1916.
C39 *Cambridge Magazine* 10 February 1917.
C40 *Nation* (London) 3 March 1917.
C41 *Carthusian* April 1917.
C43 *Living Age* 21 April 1917.
C44 *Colour* May 1918.
C48 *New Statesman* 21 September 1918.
C49 *Literary Digest* 16 November 1918.
C51 *New Statesman* 11 January 1919.
C53 *Reveille* February 1919.
C54 *Land and Water* 6 February 1919.
C55 *Land and Water* 20 February 1919.
C56 *Literary Digest* 8 March 1919.
C57 *New Statesman* 22 March 1919.
C63 *Living Age* 10 May 1919.
C194 *Nation and Athenaeum* 12 July 1924.
C216 *Southwest Review* July 1925.
C221 *Nation and Athenaeum* 24 October 1925.
C248 *Saturday Review of Literature* 18 December 1926.
C308 *New Writing and Daylight* (Summer) 1943.
C827 *Daily Express* 9 November 1967.

'War Poetry in This War' appeared in *The Listener* 23 October 1940, and was reprinted as 'The Poets of World War II' in *The Common Asphodel.* London: Hamish Hamilton, 1949.

VARIANTS OF THE POEMS
The following notes mostly cover the variants of the poems in Graves' books. The variants which appeared in magazines are not shown. In general, only differences of content are given; changes in typography, which are common, are not.

Some manuscripts of the poems are present in Graves'
letters to Sir Edward Marsh and to Siegfried Sassoon.
Variants in these are only noted when the contents are
significantly different.

In the Shadow of Death
In Graves' library copy of *Over the Brazier*, he notes that v. 2,
l. 3 was rewritten by Sassoon. It originally read 'very, very
young'.

A Renascence
In answer to Marsh's suggestions for *Over the Brazier:*
' "Poetry" instead of "English Art", after that thrust about
Chilton Brook, certainly.'

Limbo
A holograph copy was included with a letter to Marsh dated
October 1915. Major differences are as follows:

l. 9   And the dying whisper 'parapets too low . . .
l. 10 Collect those bodies . . . quick . . . build them up there'

l. 13 Babies like tickling and the violin
l. 14 Goes softly . . . Is this Limbo I've fall'n in?

In answer to Marsh's suggestions for *Over the Brazier:*
'Right Ho!

                         . . . sunny cornland where
        Babies like tickling and where tall white horses . . .'

The First Funeral
A holograph copy was included with a letter to Marsh dated
October 1915. No major differences occur.

The Adventure
A holograph copy was included with a letter to Marsh dated
October 1915. No major differences occur.
    In answer to Marsh's suggestions for *Over the Brazier:* 'Yes,
"she'd dragged him home".'

I Hate the Moon
A holograph copy was included with a letter to Marsh dated
October 1915. No major differences occur.

Big Words
In answer to Marsh's suggestions for *Over the Brazier:* 'Quite right. The "Being in my present mood" I put in before Loos as a sop to Nemesis. When I wrote the epilogue after the show I forgot to remove the qualifications. How about:

> . . . feel small sorrow
> Confess no sins and make weak delays . . .?'

The original manuscript is missing.

The Dead Fox Hunter
In answer to Marsh's suggestions for *Over the Brazier:* 'I put "taste" in the singular because "tastes" is such a horribly sibilant word. A redundancy of sis is my *bête noire.* I'd sacrifice even grammar and sense to prevent this—If you listen to the line:

> . . . Serves all tastes, or what's for him to do?

you can imagine how I object to taste in the plural. It was yourself, Eddie, who taught me to listen to the sound of the line instead of scanning with the eye!

"In hunting" is wrong, but I didn't want to use "still" in the old English sense if I can help it. Why not change the preposition to "at"

> . . .At hunting died,

That's English enough, isn't it?'

The original manuscript is missing.

It's a Queer Time
The last three verses are contained in a letter dated 22 May 1915 to Marsh, with many differences. Only major differences are shown below:

v. 3, l. 3 You fall but feel no sort of pain
v. 3, l. 8 Ah, this is a queer time
v. 4, l. 3 You're choking, choking, then hallo!
v. 4, l. 8 Ah, this is a queer time
v. 5, l. 4 But fellows do object to passing straight
v. 5, l. 6 To Alleluiahs and the full rich chime
v. 5, l. 7 Of Golden bells
> They swear and say
v. 5, l. 8 'By God, it's a queer time.'

In answer to Marsh's suggestions for *Over the Brazier:* 'All right—I expect you're right about the rhythm, so we'll have

> ... Alleluiah-chanting and the chime

which is a bit richer and stronger than your suggestion "Alleluiah-singing" and has the rhythm.'

1915
Appeared in C35 as 'Between La Bassée and Béthune'.

Over the Brazier
In A1a verses 3 and 4 are:

> But Willy said: 'No, Home's played out:
>   Old England's quite a hopeless place:
>   I've lost all feeling for my race:
> The English stay-at-home's a tout,
> A cad; I've done with him for life.
> I'm off to Canada with my wee wife.

> 'Come with us, Mac, old thing,' but Mac
>   Drawled: 'No, a Coral Isle for me,
>   A warm green jewel in the South Sea.
> Of course you'll sneer, and call me slack,
> And Colonies are quite jolly ... but—
> Give me my hot beach and my cocoanut.'

A1b contains the final version.

In answer to Marsh's suggestions for *Over the Brazier:* 'Log-hut, certainly.'

The Bough of Nonsense
There is a holograph version of this poem dated 13 August 1916 among Sassoon's letters, with the following differences:

> v. 3, l. 4 'Like Saints upborne by Seraphim'
> v. 5, l. 4 'Of course a roof of pig iron often falls
> v. 5, l. 5 when jam and putty go to build the walls.'

The first 'S.' and 'R.' appear as 'S.S.' and 'R.G.'

Goliath and David
In A2 it is not divided into stanzas, and the poem begins:

> Once an earlier David took
> Smooth pebbles from the brook:

In A3 the poem begins:

> Yet once an earlier David took
> Smooth pebbles from the brook:

The Last Post
In A2 it includes an additional two-line stanza:

> The music ceased and the red sunset flare
> Was blood about his head as he stood there.

A Dead Boche
In A23 and A24 only a part of the poem appears, and it is included at the end of 'Familiar Letter to Siegfried Sassoon'. The fragment included at the end of 'Letter' is:

> . . . today I found in Mametz wood
> A certain cure for lust of blood,

The second verse is the same.

Escape
In A2, l. 8 is 'with fine stars' for 'in fine stars' and l. 28 is 'Tickler's jam' for 'ration jam'. In A3 the final version appears.

There is a holograph version of this dated 9 August 1916 among Sassoon's letters, which reads:

> TO S. S. WHO MOURNED ME DEAD
> But Sassons I *was* dead an hour or more.
> I woke when I'd already passed the door
> Where Cerberus guards, and half-way down the road
> To Lethe, as the crazy sign post showed.
> I felt the vapours of forgetfulness
> Float in my nostrils, and may heaven bless
> The discoverer of gas-helmets: Quick as thought
> I dragged mine on, and rolling sideways caught
> And overthrew my bearers, and so back
> Breathless with leaping heart . . .

and

> Bellows, hurls stones . . . not even a honeyed cake,
> 'God dog . . . Good Cerberus . . . for pity's sake ... .'
> Ah, a great luminous thought! . . .

In l. 29 'with ration jam' is crossed out and 'in Tickler's jam' is substituted.

Not Dead

In a letter to Marsh dated 4 April 1916, there is a version that reads:

Walking through trees to cool my heat and pain,
I know that David's with me here again:
All that is simple, happy and strong, he is.
Wood burns with a pleasant smoke
Rising in thick curls—so were his!
Caressingly I stroke
Rough bark of the sturdy oak:
I laugh at chaffinch and at primroses.
Over the whole wood in a little while
Breaks his slow smile.

The Legion

A3, l. 16 'struggle' for 'straggle' and l. 23 'God damn it' for 'Hell take it'.

To R. N.

In A3 the title is 'To Robert Nichols' and in l. 6 'for your desire' rather than 'at your desire'.

An earlier version appears in a letter to Robert Nichols dated 2 February 1917:

TO ROBERT WHO'D HAVE ME FEED HIS FAUN WITH CHERRIES

Like a sad bittern, I
Sing to you mournfully.
Here by a snow bound river
In scrapen holes we shiver,
Why should your poet rhyme
June grass and summer ease,
Sleek fauns and cherry time,
Vague music and green trees,
And Life born young again
For your gay goatish brute
Drunk with warm melodies
Singing on banks of thyme,
Lips dark with juicy stain
Ears hung with bobbing fruit?
No, Robert, there's small reason;
Cherries are out of season.

Ice grips at branch and root
And all the birds are mute.

Familiar Letter to Siegfried Sassoon
In A3 the title is 'Letter to S. S. from Mametz Wood', with the following changes:

st. 1, l. 4 'For jolly old' for 'For golden-houred'
st. 2, l. 13 'jolly' for 'mountain'
st. 2, l. 31 'Ben and Claire once' for 'three young children'
st. 3, l. 18 'Welch-ski' for 'foreign'
st. 3, l. 19 'we' for 'they'
st. 3, l. 20 'us vocal' for 'them tuneful'

The third stanza is divided into three after the eighth and sixteenth lines.

In Graves' library copy of A23, ll. 17–22 and ll. 24–28 in the second stanza are marked in pencil 'omit' and st. 3, l. 18 'foreign' is changed back to 'Welch-ski' as in A3.

Corporal Stare
In A3, l. 13 'jolly' for 'mighty'.

Through the Periscope
This poem was never published. A holograph copy was sent to Marsh in a letter dated October 1915.

In answer to Marsh's suggestions for *Over the Brazier:* 'I quite agree "Through the Periscope" should go.'

Died of Wounds
This poem was never published. A holograph copy was sent to Marsh in a letter dated 18 October 1915.

The Savage Story of Cardonette
This poem was never published. A holograph copy was sent to Marsh in a letter dated 14 August 1916.

The Patchwork Quilt
This poem was never published. It was included in a letter to Sassoon on 9 July 1918.

The Leveller
In A5, v. 2, l. 2 'Girlish' for 'Blue-eyed', and the poem ends with:

To cheer the womenfolk of each.

In Graves' library copy of A5, v. 1, l. 1 'that' is changed to 'one' and v. 1, l. 3 'one' is changed to 'a'. The last four lines are added (in ink).

Sergeant-Major Money
Substantial changes occurred when this was reprinted in A73. The original version in A16 was:

It wasn't our battalion, but we lay alongside it,
    So the story is as true as the allegory's frank.
They hadn't one Line-officer left, after Arras,
    Except a sick Major and a Colonel who drank.

'B' Company Commander didn't think enough or know
        enough
    To care for his men; he had much else to do.
So Sergeant-Major Money 'carried on', as instructed,
    And his ways, fellow-democrats, would astonish you.

His Old Army humour was so well-spiced and hearty
    That one youngster shot himself and one lost his wits;
But discipline's maintained, and back in rest-billets,
    The Colonel congratulates 'B' Company on its kits.

The subalterns went easy, as was easy for subalterns
    With a power like Money driving the machine;
But finally two Welshmen, pit-boys from the Rhondda,
    Bayoneted their tyrant in a field-canteen.

Well, we couldn't blame the officers, they relied on Money,
    And we couldn't blame those Welshmen, their courage
        was grand.
Or, least of all, blame Money, an old stiff surviving
    In a New (bloody) Army he couldn't understand.

Officers and men were out of all touch,
    So Money carried on, what else could he do,
A go-between left as a law to himself?
    Distress and revolt, were these anything new?

In A73, v. 2, l. 2 'shell-fish' for 'gas drill'.

Armistice Day, 1918

On 28 November 1918 Graves wrote to Marsh, 'I'll send you those poems revised in case you'd like to show them to Ivor [Novello] "Pot & Kettle" & "Hawk & Buckle" and a little squib called "Nov 11th" thrown in for fun.'

NOV 11TH

Why are they cheering and shouting
   What's all the scurry of feet
With little boys banging on keetle and can
   Wild-laughter of girls in the street?

——————

O those are the fresh of the city,
   The thoughtless and ignorant scum
Who hang out the bunting when war is let loose
   And for victory bang on a drum.

But the boys who are killed in the battle
   Who fought with no rage and no rant,
Are peacefully sleeping on pallets of mud,
   Low down with the worm and the ant.

The line after the first verse is included in the manuscript and seems to indicate there were others.

When Graves published the poem in C827, in 1967, he called it 'November 11th, 1918'. The present title appeared in A127.

A Letter from Wales

In A16, l. 81 'as ill or wounded' for 'that time, as wounded'.

Recalling War

In A50, st. 3, l. 5 'tasteless' for 'tasty'.

COLOPHON

This volume is revised slightly from the first edition published in England in 1988. The editor has included an addendum with four additional poems and made minor changes to the notations. The text of this book was set in Walbaum Monotype. The front matter was set in Bembo in keeping with the series.

Composed by Books, Deatsville, Alabama.

The book was printed by Princeton University Press, Lawrenceville, New Jersey on acid free paper.

This is part of a series of Robert Graves books. Other titles in the series include IN BROKEN IMAGES: Selected Correspondence (1914–1946); BETWEEN MOON AND MOON: Selected Correspondence (1946–1972); THE GREEK MYTHS; THE HEBREW MYTHS; and THE NAZARENE GOSPEL RESTORED.